A

RUDOLF STEINER (1861–1925) called his spiritual philosophy 'anthroposophy', meaning 'wisdom of the human being'. As a highly developed seer, he based his work on direct knowledge and perception of spiritual dimensions. He initiated a modern and universal 'science of spirit', accessible to anyone willing to exercise clear and unprejudiced thinking.

From his spiritual investigations Steiner provided suggestions for the renewal of many activities, including education (both general and special), agriculture, medicine, economics, architecture, science, philosophy, religion and the arts. Today there are thousands of schools, clinics, farms and other organizations involved in practical work based on his principles. His many published works feature his research into the spiritual nature of the human being, the evolution of the world and humanity, and methods of personal development. Steiner wrote some 30 books and delivered over 6000 lectures across Europe. In 1924 he founded the General Anthroposophical Society, which today has branches throughout the world.

AN EXERCISE FOR KARMIC INSIGHT

RUDOLF STEINER

Sophia Books

Rudolf Steiner Press
Hillside House, The Square
Forest Row RH18 5ES

www.rudolfsteinerpress.com

Published by Rudolf Steiner Press 2007

First published by Rudolf Steiner Press in 1956 as part of
Karmic Relationships, Esoteric Studies, Vol. II

This translation revised by Pauline Wehrle
© Rudolf Steiner Press 2007

Originally published in German as part of the volume entitled
Esoterische Betrachtungen karmischer Zusammenhänge (volume
236 in the *Rudolf Steiner Gesamtausgabe* or Collected Works)
by Rudolf Steiner Verlag, Dornach. This authorized translation
is published by permission of the Rudolf Steiner
Nachlassverwaltung, Dornach

A catalogue record for this book is available from the British
Library

ISBN 978 185584 154 3

Cover by Andrew Morgan
Typeset by DP Photosetting, Neath, West Glamorgan
Printed and bound in Great Britain by Cromwell Press Limited,
Trowbridge, Wiltshire

Contents

We shall begin today to consider the inner soul activities that can lead people gradually to have conceptions, thoughts about karma. These thoughts, these views will open them to the possibility of seeing from a karmic point of view experiences of theirs caused by karma.

When we look around in our human environment, what we human beings actually see of the physical world is only what is caused by physical force in a physical way. And if we do see something in the physical world that is not caused by physical forces we still see it by means of external physical substance, external physical objects of perception. Of course, when people do something out of their own will this is not caused by physical forces, by physical causes, for in many respects it comes out of the free will.

But all that we perceive outwardly is entirely of the nature of the world's physical sense phenomena, and this is how we observe it. In the entire sphere of what we observe in this way it is not possible for us to become aware of the karmic connection of an experience we ourselves go through. For the whole picture of this karmic connection has its existence in the spiritual world, is in fact inscribed in what is the etheric world [the world of life], the basis of the astral outer world [the world of soul], or the world of those spiritual beings who inhabit this astral outer world. None of this is seen as long as we merely direct our senses to the physical world. So all that we perceive in the physical world is perceived through our senses. These senses are active without our being able to do much about it. Our eyes perceive impressions of light and of colour without acquiring much help from us. We can at the most—and even that is half involuntary—turn our gaze in a particular direction, or we can either look at something or turn away. Even when doing this a great part of it is unconscious, though there is at least a little bit of consciousness involved. And when we think about what our eyes have to do inside to see colour, the extraordinarily wise and wonderful inner activity which has to be performed whenever we see anything—as human beings we could never achieve this if we were supposed to do it consciously. That would be totally out of the question. All this must for the time being happen unconsciously, because it is much too wise for human beings to be able to do anything about it in any way.

To acquire the right view concerning an understanding of the human being, we must make ourselves fully aware of all the wise ways things are arranged in the world and which we cannot do ourselves. If people confine themselves to thinking only of what they themselves can do, they are actually blocking their way to knowledge. The path to knowledge really begins at the point where we realize, with the greatest humility, all that we are incapable of doing, and which nevertheless has to happen in the course of life. Our eyes, our ears, in fact all our sense organs, are in reality such profoundly wise instruments that human beings will need to study them for a long time before we will be able even to have an inkling of an understanding of them during our lifetime. We should focus our full attention on this. The spiritual aspect of things, however, cannot be observed in such an unconscious manner. In earlier times in human evolution this applied also to observing the spiritual; there was an instinctive clairvoyance, which has now faded away in the course of humanity's evolution.

From now onwards human beings have consciously to take up a position with regard to the cosmos from where they will be able to penetrate the spiritual. For we will have to penetrate into the spiritual element if we are to grasp the karmic connections of any experience we may have.

Now it all depends, at least where observing

karma is concerned, on our beginning to pay attention to what can happen within us in order to acquire the faculty of observing karmic relationships. We on our part have to do a little towards these observations consciously. We must do more in fact than we do for our eyes, for example, in order to become conscious of colour. What we have to learn here first of all, my dear friends, can be put into one word: wait. We must learn to wait. We have to be able to wait for the inner experiences.

I have spoken before about being able to wait. It was about the year 1889—I shall also include this in my *Autobiography*[1]—that I first became aware of the spiritual structure of Goethe's fairy tale of *The Green Snake and the Beautiful Lily*. And that was the first time that as it were the perception of a further relationship, a larger one than is given in the fairy tale itself, came to me. But I also knew at that moment: I cannot yet make of this relationship what I will one day be able to make of it. And so the perception the fairy tale had awakened in me at that time remained dormant within me.

It welled up once more in 1896, seven years later, but again it was not in the kind of way that it could be properly formed; and it did so again seven years after that, in about 1903. Even then, although it came quite clearly, and in connection with other things, it still did not lend itself to being put into form. It was not until seven years later again, when I conceived my first Mystery Play, *The Portal of Initiation*,[2] that the fairy tale reappeared, transformed in such a way that it could be pliably shaped and formed.

Such things, then, really have to be waited for, for they require time to mature. We must bring our own experiences into relation with what exists out there in the world. At the moment when a plant is still at the seed stage, we obviously cannot already have the whole plant. We have to give the seed the right conditions for it to begin to grow, then we must wait until the blossom and then the fruit develop from it. And we have to do the same thing with the experiences we go through. We cannot allow ourselves to take the line of being thrilled by an experience simply because it has happened, and then forget about it. People who only want their experiences while they are fresh and still present will be able to do very little about seeing in the spiritual world. We must be able to wait. We must be able to give experiences the opportunity to mature in our soul.

Now there is the possibility of a comparatively quick maturing of insight into karmic relationships if, for a considerable time, we try patiently and with inner energy to picture with greater and greater consciousness an experience which would otherwise simply take its course, without being properly grasped, and fade away in the course of life. This is what usually happens to events. For what do people do with the events and experiences that happen to them all day? They actually only *half* notice them. You can form a picture of experiences only being half noticed if you sit down one day in the afternoon or the evening—and I advise you to do this—and ask yourself: What actually happened to me at half-past nine this morning? And now try to call up what you experienced in every detail as though it were actually happening, say at half-past seven in the evening—as if you were placing it in front of you as an invisible, spiritual work of art. You will see how much will be missing, how much you did not notice, and how difficult this is to do. If you pick up a pen or a pencil to write it down you will soon begin to bite your pencil, because you cannot remember the details, and in the last resort you hope to bite them out of the pencil!

But the whole point is that you have to start by setting yourself the task of picturing for yourself, as precisely as possible, something you have experienced, not at the moment it is actually happening, but afterwards. You must make a picture of it as though you were trying to paint it in spirit. And if the experience is one in which somebody spoke, this must be made as graphic as possible: the sound of their voice, the way in which the words were used distinctly or clumsily and so on. Do this with strength and energy—in other words, you put into the picture all that you experienced. If you construct a picture like this of something you have experienced during the day then the following night your astral body,[3] when it is outside your physical body and etheric body, occupies itself with this picture. The astral body itself is in reality the bearer of the picture, and it shapes it outside the body. The astral body takes the picture with it when it goes out on the first night. And it shapes it out there when it is outside the physical and etheric body.

That is the first stage (we will follow these stages quite exactly): the sleeping astral body, outside the physical and etheric body, shapes the picture of the experience. Where does it do this? It does this in the external ether, for where it now is is in the external ether world.

Picture to yourselves the human being. The

physical and etheric body lie in bed, and the astral body is outside. We will disregard the ego. There outside is the astral body reproducing this picture you have made. But it does this in the external ether, and in consequence of this the following happens.

Picture it to yourselves. The astral body is outside [lightly shaded].[4] Now it shapes the picture out there, which I will draw like this [inner shading, red]—this is of course purely diagrammatic. All this happens in the external ether, and this encrusts, as it were, with its own

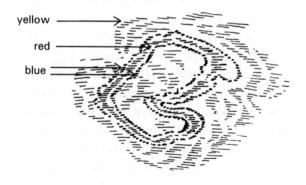

yellow

red

blue

substance the picture shaped in the astral body. That is, the outer ether makes an entire etheric form (blue), which is seen as an extremely sharp picture by the eye of the spirit.

In the morning you return to your physical and etheric body and bring into them what has been given substance by the external ether. That is to say the sleeping astral body shapes, when outside the physical and etheric body, the picture of the experience, and the external ether then impregnates the picture with its own substance. You can imagine that this has made the picture stronger, and that now, when the astral body returns in the morning with this more substantial form, it can make an impression on your etheric body. It does this now with the help of forces derived from the outer ether. The second stage, therefore, is: the astral body impresses the picture into your etheric body.

These were the events of the first day and the first night. [See summary, page 18.] Now we come to the second day. On the second day, while you are busying yourself with all the little things of life in full waking consciousness, there, below consciousness, in the unconscious, the picture is descending into the etheric body. And during the next night, when the astral body has gone out again and the etheric body is undisturbed, the etheric body elaborates this picture. So during the second night the picture is worked on by your own etheric body. So the second stage is that the astral body impresses during the day the picture into the etheric body and the etheric body elaborates the picture during the night. This, then, is the second day and the second night. [See summary.]

Now if you do this, if you are actually not above continuing to occupy yourself with the picture you formed the preceding day—and you can go on working on it for a reason which I shall mention in a moment—you will continue to have a living relationship with it.

What does this mean—to continue occupying

yourself with it? If you really make an effort on the first day, after you had the experience, to shape such a picture vigorously, forming it flexibly with strong, characteristic lines, you have really exerted yourself mentally. Such things demand mental exertion. I am sorry, but I am not dropping a hint—present company is, of course, always excepted!—yet it has to be said that most people simply do not know what mental exertion is. For mental exertion, real mental exertion, has to be a soul activity. If you allow the world to have the kind of effect on you where thoughts take their course without your taking them in hand then you are not exerting yourself mentally. Getting tired does not mean that you have made any mental effort. You must not imagine that when something makes you tired that you have been exerting your mind. Reading can tire you, for instance. But if you are not being actively productive in some way while you are reading, but only let the thoughts in the book run through your mind, then you are of course not exerting yourself. On the other hand, people who have really been making an effort, who have exerted themselves out of an inner activity of soul, may then take up a book, a very interesting one, and just 'sleep off' their spiritual exertion in the best possible way. Naturally we can fall asleep over a book if we are tired. This type of getting tired is no sign at all of mental exertion.

A sign of mental exertion, however, is that the brain feels worn out, just as when you have been using your arm a lot for lifting you feel that a demand has been made on your arm muscles. Ordinary thinking does not have such an effect on the brain. But this stays with you, and you will even notice that when you do this the first time, then the second, the third, the tenth, you get a slight headache. Not that you are getting tired or falling asleep—on the contrary. You cannot fall asleep, but will far more likely get a slight headache. Only you must certainly not think of this headache as something detestable but as an actual proof of the fact that you have exerted your head.

Well, the effect continues, and it goes on affecting you until you have gone to sleep. If you have really done this during the day you will wake up in the morning with the feeling that there is actually something in you! 'I do not quite know what it is, but there is something in me that wants something of me. In fact, it is not such an indifferent matter that I worked on this picture yesterday, but it really does mean something. For this picture has changed. Today the picture is giving me quite different feelings from any I have had before; the picture is making me have quite specific feelings.'

This experience remains with you the following day. And the feeling this gives you, and which you cannot get rid of throughout the day, is a witness to the fact that the picture is now descending into your etheric body, as I have described, and that the etheric body is absorbing it.

Now when you wake up after the next night it will probably happen to you, when you slip back into your body after these two days [see summary] that you find this picture somewhat changed, transformed. The moment you wake up the next morning you find it within you again, and it appears as a very real dream. But it has gone through a transformation; it has not remained the same but has undergone a change. It will go through a number of changes until it has become something different. It will take on the appearance as if spiritual beings were there in some form, bringing you this experience. And you do, virtually, get the impression that this experience you have made a picture of in this way was actually bestowed on you. If it had been an experience together with another human being you would then be left with the feeling that you had not actually experienced that only through that person, but that it was presented to you. Other powers, spiritual ones, have been involved; it was these who brought it to you.

Now the following day arrives. And on this day the picture is carried down from the etheric body into the physical body. The etheric body impresses this picture into the physical body, right into the nerve processes, the blood processes. On the third day the picture is impressed into the physical body. So the third stage is: the etheric body stamps the picture into the physical body.

And now comes the next night. You have been attending throughout the day to the ordinary little trifles of life and underneath it all the important process has been taking place of the picture being carried down into the physical body. This has been going on in the sub-conscious. And when the following night arrives the picture is elaborated in the physical body. In the physical body it is spiritualized. First of all, during the day this picture is brought down into the processes of the blood and of the nerves, but in the night it is spiritualized. Those with spiritual sight see this picture being worked on by the physical body, but it appears spiritually as an altogether changed picture. We could describe it by saying that during the following night the physical body elaborates the picture.

First day and first night: When outside the physical and etheric body the astral body shapes the picture of the experience. The outer ether impregnates the picture with its own substance.

Second day and second night: The picture is stamped by the astral body into the etheric body. Then the etheric body elaborates the picture in the course of the next night.

Third day and third night: The picture is stamped by the etheric body into the physical body. Then

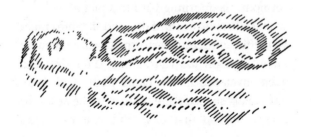

the physical body elaborates the picture during the next night.

Now this is something you must visualize absolutely exactly. The physical body really elaborates this picture spiritually, it spiritualizes it. So that if you have really gone through all this, then whilst you are asleep what happens is that the physical body actually elaborates the whole thing, but it now no longer remains within the physical body. There arises out of the physical body a transformed version, a greatly magnified transformation of the picture. And when you get up in the morning this picture is there, with you actually floating in it. It is like a kind of cloud that you yourself are within. You get up in the morning with this picture.

This, then, is the third day and the third night. With this entirely transformed picture you get out of bed on the fourth day. You rise from sleep enveloped in this cloud [red]. And if you have really shaped the picture with the necessary energy on the first day, and you have paid

19

attention to what kind of feeling you had on the second day, you will now notice that the present picture is filled with your will. It contains will! But this will is unable to come to expression—it is as though it were shackled. Expressed somewhat radically, it is as if an incredibly daring sprinter had resolved to make a display of a bravado race—and he imagines he is sprinting. I am sprinting down to upper Dornach in my imagination, my will is already engaged. But at the very moment I want to start moving and the will is strongest, somebody holds me back so that I stand there rigidly. My whole will is set to go, but I cannot make it function. The process is more or less like that.

When you have this experience of feeling yourself as though being put in a vice—for you do feel as though clamped in a vice after the third night—when you wake up again with this feeling of being caught in a vice with your will thoroughly shackled, then—if you can be attentive to this—the will becomes transformed:

the will becomes *seeing*. The will cannot do anything, but it leads to your being able to see something. It becomes an eye of the soul, and the picture you woke up with becomes actual, objective. What you see is the event of the previous earth life, or of some previous earth life, which had been the cause of what we sketched as a picture on the first day. By way of their transformation through feeling and will we arrive at the picture of the causal event of a proceeding incarnation.

When we describe these things they appear somewhat overpowering. This is not surprising, for they are utterly unfamiliar to people of the present time. But they were not so unknown to people of earlier cultural epochs. Only, according to the opinion of modern people who are so clever, those earlier people, in their whole way of life, were stupid. Nevertheless, these 'stupid' people of earlier cultural eras really had these experiences, only modern human beings cloud everything over with their intellects, which make them clever but do not make them wise exactly.

As I say, the matter seems somewhat tumultuous, when one relates it this way. But one is obliged, after all, to use such words. For since these things are quite unknown today, if more gentle words were used their real nature would not come across so cleverly. This has to come across without hesitation. All the same, the whole experience, from beginning to end, that I have described as taking place over three days must take its course in intimate inwardness, in all calmness and equanimity. For so-called occult experiences—and these are such—are not the kind of thing that can be bragged about. If one begins to brag about them they immediately stop. They really have to take place in inner peace and composure. And it is best if, for the time being, nobody knows anything about what is going on except the person concerned.

Now you must not think that the exercise succeeds immediately at the first attempt. One always finds that people like it when exercises such as this one are described. This is quite understandable, and is a good thing that this is so. What a lot of new experiences one will be able to have! And people set about it with enthusiastic devotion. They begin, but it doesn't work. Then they become thoroughly disheartened. Then perhaps they try it several more times. Again they do not succeed. But if someone has tried it about 49 times or somebody else 69 times then the fiftieth or the seventieth time they do it they do succeed. For what really matters with all these exercises is that one begins to acquire a kind of habit in one's soul. The first thing one must do is to find one's way into these things, and acquire habits of soul. And this is actually something one should take careful note of in the Anthroposophical Society which, since the Christmas Foundation,[5] should be a full expression of the Anthroposophical Movement.

Really a very great deal has been given out in

the Anthroposophical Society. It is enough to make one giddy when one sees the rows of lecture courses that have been printed. But in spite of this people come to me again and again asking one thing or another. In the majority of cases this is not necessary at all, for if people really worked on what is contained in the lecture cycles then most of the questions would be answered by themselves in a much surer way. One just has to have the patience to do this. Patience is all you need. Indeed, anthroposophical literature contains in many ways a great deal that can work on in the soul. And out of the esoteric understanding that now exists we will find the heart for what has to be accomplished, and the time will be well filled with the things that have to be done. But, on the other hand, with regard to many of the things which people want to know, it must be pointed out that a lot of old lecture courses are in existence which are not being read any more, and that the most people say about them is that they want them followed by 'new' ones. These things are closely related to what I have been talking about right now.

One does not acquire the inner stability to pursue the process germinating and ripening in one's soul if there is this desire to hurry from one new thing to another; the essential point is that things have to mature in the soul. First and foremost we must try to break ourselves of a habit that for the most part is the normal condition today. We must accustom ourselves to inner, active soul work, work that engages the spirit. This is the kind of thing that is going to help to make a success of winning through to the final stage of transformation of an experience one wants to understand karmically.

This is the way we have to set about things if we want to understand spiritual matters. Right from the start we have to tell ourselves: the moment we turn our thoughts to the spirit we have made a beginning. What is impossible is to expect an immediate result; we have to be able to wait. Supposing I experience something that is caused by karma in a previous life, then it is like this [Dr Steiner does the following drawing]:

I am here [right]. Here is the experience I had today. This is caused by the quite differently constituted personality in the same ego in a previous incarnation [left]. There it is. It has long ceased to belong to my personality, but it has been inscribed into the etheric world or respectively the astral world lying behind the etheric world. Now I have first of all to retrace my steps and go back the way I came. I told you that to start with things seem as if someone were actually bringing the experience to me. This is how it is on the second day. But after the third day the situation is that those who brought it to me, those spiritual beings, withdraw, and I become aware of it as something of my own which I myself, in a previous incarnation, laid down as a cause. And because this is of course no longer in the present and because it is something I have to look at as being in the past earth life, therefore I appear to myself, because I am part of it, as though I am shackled. This state of being shackled does not cease until, having perceived the event, I have a picture of what was in the past incarnation, and then look back again at the event, which I have not lost sight of throughout these three days. By coming back to the present I am free once more, for the effect makes me free to move. While I am pinned down solely in the cause, I cannot move about in it. Stepping back into a previous incarnation I am as though shackled by the cause, and only when I now enter this incarnation are the shackles removed again.

Let us take an example. Suppose someone experiences at a particular time on a certain day that a friend says something to him that is not altogether pleasant—perhaps he had not expected it. Well now, he clearly pictures to himself how he felt when he listened to what his friend said. He makes a really vivid picture of what he went through, the slight shock it gave him, how he got a bit annoyed, even offended. This is an inner effect, and as such it must be brought into the picture.

Now he lets the three days run their course. On the second day he goes about saying to himself: 'The picture I formed yesterday has had a remarkable effect on me. All day today I have a kind of sour feeling, of being in a bad mood, as though I had a tummy upset. I have never before felt the sort of thing that is coming from this picture. At the end of the whole process, on the morning after the third day, I wake up and have the definite feeling that this picture is having the effect of shackling me. Then I become aware of the event from the past incarnation; I see it in front of me. I pass from this to the experience that is still quite fresh, still intact. The shackling stops, and I realize, 'Aha, so this is how things were in the previous incarnation!' This is what caused it; and now the effect is here. With this I can live again—the thing is present once more.'

This must be practised again and again, for usually the thread breaks at the first attempt on the very first day. And then nothing follows. It is particularly good if you can let these things run alongside one another, and do not limit yourself to *one* event, but bring a number of events of the day into picture form in this way. You will say: 'Then I must live the next day with all kinds of different feelings.' And so you can. It does no harm at all. Just try it; these things go quite well together. 'And after the third day must I then be shackled a number of times?' This does no harm either. None of this matters. The things will sort themselves out. What belongs to the present incarnation from a previous one will find its way to it.

But it just will not succeed at the first attempt—the thread breaks. We must have the patience to do this over and over again. Then you feel something growing stronger in your soul. You feel something awakening in the soul, so that you actually say to yourself: 'Up to now you were only filled with blood, all you felt pulsating in you was blood and breath. Now it is as though there was something within you besides blood. You are filled with something else as well.'

You can even have the feeling you are filled with something of which you can quite definitely say that it is like a metal that has become aeriform. You actually feel something like metal within you. You cannot describe it any other way than this. You feel metal spreading throughout your body. Just as you can say of a particular kind of drinking water that it tastes metallic, the whole body seems to 'taste' as though it were permeated by some delicate substance, which in reality however is a spiritual element.

You notice this when you come upon something which was, of course, always there in you, but of which you are now for the first time becoming aware. And this experience gives you courage again. For if the thread keeps on breaking and things are just as they were—if you want to get hold of a karmic connection, but the thread is always breaking—you could lose your courage. But when you have this feeling of what you are filled with, then you take courage again. And you tell yourself that you will succeed in due course. But, my dear friends, these things have to be gone through in an absolutely calm and peaceful mood. Those who cannot do these exercises calmly and peacefully, but get excited and emotional, are spreading an inner fog over what really ought to happen, and nothing comes of it.

It could be said that there are certain people out there who know of anthroposophy only from hearsay, who have perhaps read none at all or only what opponents have written. It is getting very funny. Many of the opponents' writings spring up just like mushrooms—they quote literature, but among the literature they quote there are none of my books at all, but only books written by opponents! The authors admit that they have not actually approached the original sources, but only know the antagonistic literature. Such things exist today. And so there are people out there who talk about it and say, 'Oh, the anthroposophists are crazy!' As a matter of fact, what one can least of all afford to be in order to reach anything at all in the spiritual world is to be crazy. Because one must not be crazy in the very slightest degree if one hopes to attain something in the spiritual world. And being a tiny bit crazy is a hindrance to attaining anything. This must be avoided. One must not be the slightest bit crotchety or moody. For any giving way to a passing mood puts nothing but obstacles in the way of any kind of progress in the spiritual world. If you want to make headway in the field of anthroposophy there is nothing for it but to have an absolutely sane head and an absolutely sane heart. Raving about something is already starting to go crazy, and this way you will achieve nothing.

The kind of things I have been telling you about today, however strange they sound, must be experienced with absolute sober mindedness, absolute soundness of head and of heart. Truly, there is nothing that can more surely save you from the slightest daily attack of madness than anthroposophy. People would be cured of all their madness by anthroposophy if they would only devote themselves to it really intensively. If someone were to set himself to go a little crazy just with the help of anthroposophy, he would most certainly find it was unfit for the task!

But I am not joking when I say this. The reason I am saying it is because this must also be an integral part of the character of anthroposophical endeavour. This is the attitude we must adopt to the matter—as I have just explained to you half jokingly—if we want to approach it in the right way, with the right orientation. We must set out to be as sane as possible; then we approach it with the right attitude. We can at least aim for this, and especially where the crazy little things of life are concerned.

I was once friends with a very clever professor of philosophy, now long since dead, who used to say on every occasion: 'We all show a bit of spleen!' Meaning we all have our moments of being in a bad mood. But he was a very intelligent man; so I always believed there was something behind his words, that his assertion was not altogether without foundation! He did not become an anthroposophist...

Notes

The text is a record of a lecture Rudolf Steiner gave to members of the Anthroposophical Society in Dornach on 9 May 1924.

GA = *Gesamtausgabe*: the Collected Works of Rudolf Steiner in the original German.

1. GA 28. *Autobiography*, (latest edition) SteinerBooks 2006.
2. Steiner's four Mystery Plays are published in *Four Mystery Dramas*, Rudolf Steiner Press 1997 (GA 14).
3. Steiner gives a full description of the various bodies of the human being in his book *Theosophy*, Rudolf Steiner Press 1973 (GA 9).
4. Steiner often illustrated his lectures with coloured blackboard drawings. A selection of these are reproduced in full colour in *Blackboard Drawings, 1919–1924*, Rudolf Steiner Press 2003.

5. Rudolf Steiner refounded the Anthroposophical Society at the Christmas Foundation Meeting of 1923/24 in Dornach, Switzerland. See further in *The Christmas Conference for the Foundation of the General Anthroposophical Society*, Anthroposophic Press 1990.

Further Reading

Rudolf Steiner's fundamental books:

Knowledge of the Higher Worlds
also published as: *How to Know Higher Worlds*

Occult Science
also published as: *An Outline of Esoteric Science*

Theosophy

The Philosophy of Freedom
also published as:
Intuitive Thinking as a Spiritual Path

**Some relevant volumes of Rudolf Steiner's verses
and lectures:**

Manifestations of Karma
Karmic Relationships, Vol. II
Reincarnation and Karma
A Western Approach to Reincarnation and Karma

For all titles contact Rudolf Steiner Press (UK) or
SteinerBooks (USA):
www.rudolfsteinerpress.com www.steinerbooks.org

Publisher's Note on
Rudolf Steiner's Lectures

The lectures and addresses contained in this volume have been translated from the German, which is based on stenographic and other recorded texts that were in most cases never seen or revised by the lecturer. Hence, due to human errors in hearing and transcription, they may contain mistakes and faulty passages. Every effort has been made to ensure that this is not the case. Some of the lectures were given to audiences more familiar with anthroposophy; these are the so-called 'private' or 'members' lectures. Other lectures, like the written works, were intended for the general public. The difference between these, as Rudolf Steiner indicates in his *Autobiography*, is twofold. On the one hand, the members' lectures take for granted a background in and commitment to anthroposophy; in the public lectures this was not the case. At the same time, the members' lectures address the concerns and dilemmas of the members, while the public work speaks directly out of Steiner's own understanding of universal needs. Nevertheless, as Rudolf Steiner stresses: 'Nothing was ever said that was not solely the result of my direct experience of the growing content of anthroposophy. There was never any question of concessions to the prejudices and preferences of the members. Whoever reads these privately printed lectures can take them to represent anthroposophy in the fullest sense. Thus it was possible without hesitation—when the complaints in this direction became too persistent—to depart from the custom of circulating this material "For members only". But it must be borne in mind that faulty passages do occur in these reports not revised by myself.' Earlier in the same chapter, he states: 'Had I been able to correct them [*the private lectures*], the restriction *for members only* would have been unnecessary from the beginning.'

Other budget-priced volumes from Rudolf Steiner Press

Single lectures:
How Can I Find the Christ?
The Dead Are With Us
The Work of the Angel in Our Astral Body

Meditations:
Calendar of the Soul, The Year Participated
The Foundation Stone Meditation